If I Were a Kid in Ancient China

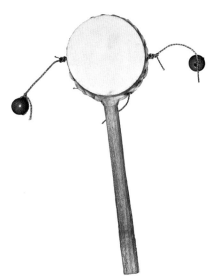

Cricket Books
Peterborough, NH

Staff

Editorial Director: Lou Waryncia

Editor: Ken Sheldon

Book Design: David Nelson, www.dnelsondesign.com

Designer: Ann Dillon

Proofreader: Eileen Terrill

Text Credits

The content of this volume is derived from articles that first appeared in *AppleSeeds, Calliope,* and *DIG* magazines. Contributing writers: Denise L. Babcock, Helen Wieman Bledsoe, Luann Hankom, Valerie Hansen, Donald James Johnson and Jean Elliott Johnson, Jane Rohan Kloecker, Kathiann M. Kowalski, Gloria Lannom, Jane Scherer, Gail Skroback Hennessey.

Picture Credits

Photos.com: cover; PhotoObjects.net: cover; StockDisc: cover; Shutterstock: cover, 1, 3, 11 (tiger), 12, 24, 25 (all); Gloria Lannom: 11 (hat, shoes); Clipart.com: 13, 14 (all), 15, 19, 28, 29; courtesy of Government Information Office, Taiwan: 16; Stock Montage: 17

Illustration Credits

Mike DiGiorgio: 4–7; Cheryl Kirk Noll: 8–10; Patty Weise: 11; Cheryl Jacobsen: 21; Wenhai Ma: 22–23; Chris Wold Dyrud: 26–27.

Library of Congress Cataloging-in-Publication Data

If I were a kid in ancient China / Lou Waryncia, editorial director; Ken Sheldon, editor.

   p. cm. — (Children of the ancient world)

   Includes index.

   ISBN-13: 978-0-8126-7931-1 (hardcover)

   ISBN-10: 0-8126-7931-8 (hardcover)

   1. China—Social life and customs—221 B.C.–960 A.D. 2. Children—China—Juvenile

literature. I. Waryncia, Lou. II. Sheldon, Ken. III. Series.

   DS748.13.I4 2006

   931—dc22   2006014671

Cricket Books

a division of Carus Publishing

30 Grove Street, Suite C

Peterborough, NH 03458

www.cricketmag.com

Printed in China

Table of Contents

Made in China

Ever wonder who came up with many of the ideas we have today? Maybe you're reading this book, which is printed on paper, with eyeglasses perched upon your nose. You can thank the Chinese for these inventions and many more.

Some people estimate that half of all basic inventions originally came from China. From the toothbrush, toothpaste, and toilet paper to a seismograph instrument for recording earthquakes, the Chinese thought of it first.

On the Block

Today, we take printed books for granted. Until the late 1400s, the only way to make books in most of the world was to hand-copy them. But

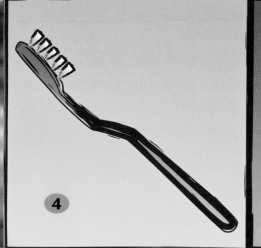

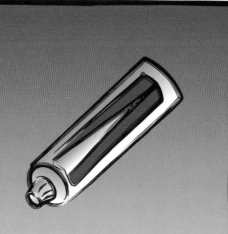

the Chinese had long used block printing. They carved words on wooden blocks, put ink on them, and pressed paper down on the blocks. This way, they could make as many copies as they wanted. Johann Gutenberg simply improved on the Chinese idea of block printing when he developed the first printing press.

Making Paper

Cai Lun of China is credited with the invention of paper in A.D. 105. His experiments involved soaking the inner bark of the mulberry tree in chemicals, then pressing it dry. Paper made from wood pulp soon became an inexpensive replacement for more expensive materials like silk, bamboo, and parchment (made from animal skins).

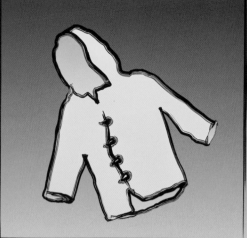

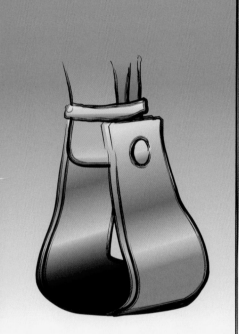

Shake, Rattle, and Roll

Back in A.D. 132, Chang Heng made a device to record earthquakes using eight copper dragons placed on fine springs around a bowl. In the center of the bowl, a metal toad sat with its mouth open. The dragons had copper balls resting in their mouths. When an earthquake occurred, the dragon closest to the source dropped its ball into the mouth of the toad.

Bug Versus Bug

Back in the third century A.D., the Chinese experimented with using insects to kill other insects and protect their mandarin oranges from harm. Today, scientists are building on this

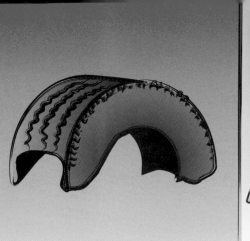

Chinese idea so they can avoid using chemicals that may hurt the environment.

The Chinese were the first to use coal for heating, and the first to build a planetarium. They invented a stirrup so soldiers could more easily mount and then stay on a horse. They also were the first to use a parachute. They invented kites (originally as a form of communication), the yo-yo, gunpowder, the compass, the wheelbarrow, the umbrella, waterproof clothing, and rubber. Add to this list the shiny pottery called porcelain, silk cloth from the cocoons of silkworms, and even the spaghetti found on your dinner plate. These are just some of the many gifts the Chinese gave to the world.

Life in Ancient China

Let's pretend you are living in China in the year A.D. 100. You are very special. In fact, all Chinese children are considered special, and your parents call you "Precious Child." Of course, old people are even more special. Your grandparents are honored for their wisdom, and you are very respectful toward them.

If you are royal, you are very wealthy. Last night, you might have fallen asleep to songs played on a stringed instrument. Today you might wear a beautiful silk brocade jacket. If you are not royal or wealthy, you may be very poor. Many Chinese peasants live on farms.

Rice growing is an important job, so you may work in a rice field.

If you're a girl, you're lucky to have been born now and not 1,000 years later. The painful practice of foot binding is not yet fashionable. But you're not completely free. Confucian teaching says that "a maiden obeys her father, a wife her husband, a widow her son." Still, there is a slight chance that you have been educated. Perhaps you have heard of the writings of Ban Zhao. She is a famous historian. The emperor has hired her to teach the empress and other ladies of the court.

As a Chinese youngster, you may have a fluffy little dog called a Chow Chow. Chow Chows have become popular in the last hundred years or so. They are one of the oldest breeds of dogs and have an unusual blue-black tongue.

You have probably heard tales of the Silk Road. Trading caravans are traveling the vast western expanses of China to bring fine silk and other goods to the "barbarians" of the Roman Empire in the West.

You may practice acrobatics, diving through flames, and tumbling from high places. Perhaps you were brought into an acrobatic troupe to train at a very young age.

You live in an exciting time, the Han dynasty. Two thousand years from now, the Chinese people will still refer to themselves as the Han people. Many new things are being invented. Perhaps you practice writing your characters on a new invention—paper. Your dinnerware may be made of delicate pottery that's made in a new way, called porcelain.

The Han government follows Confucian principles. Confucius (or Kong Fuzi) taught rules to live by that included love within the family, honesty, trustworthiness, loyalty to the government, and goodwill toward others. You know many Confucian sayings by heart, such as "He who learns but does not think is lost. He who thinks but does not learn is in great danger."

Hist-O-Bit

People in China began eating with chopsticks about 3,000 years ago. Originally, they were made of wood, bamboo, or bone.

Dressed for Success

The Chinese have always treasured children. The ancient Chinese wanted their children to be healthy, wealthy, and successful, so they took many steps to protect them from harm. They even put special designs on their clothing. The tiger was one of the most important symbols.

The Chinese word for tiger is *hu,* and *hu* also means "prosperity." The tiger was the king of land animals, and the stripes on a tiger's head look like the Chinese character for *wang,* meaning "king." By putting this symbol on their children's clothing, the Chinese hoped to frighten off evil spirits.

At the start of the hot, rainy summer season, the Chinese wore tiger charms to protect the family from disease, harmful insects, and poisons.

Some clothing showed the tiger carrying five poisonous creatures on his back—the toad, snake, centipede, scorpion, and spider or lizard. The Chinese believed that combining the five most poisonous creatures with the tiger, the most powerful animal, produced the strongest possible defense against all evils.

The Chinese character for "king" looks like the stripes on a tiger's head.

Pottery Pigs & Papier-Mâché

Thousands of years ago, children in China liked to have fun with toys, just as you do. How do we know? Because archaeologists have dug up examples of their playthings.

The ancient Chinese thought that a child who died would want his or her favorite toys in the afterlife, so they buried them with the toys. The Chinese also had superstitions about ghosts, and the parents may have offered the toys to appease the ghost of a child and keep it from coming back to haunt the family.

One of the oldest toys found so far is a two-headed pottery pig. Why a pig? Because pigs were thought to be lucky animals that provided food, just as they do in China today. Two heads meant twice as lucky.

Archaeologists have also discovered clay pottery balls and a small musical instrument that looks like an ocarina, with a mouthpiece and finger holes. Tops made of wood, clay, bamboo, or stone have turned up in places where people lived 7,000 years ago.

The story is told about the famous philosopher Laozi, who lived 2,500 years ago. He amused his parents by playing a toy drum with a handle and two strings with beads on them. When he held it by the handle and rotated it, the strings with the beads hit the drum and made a funny rattling noise.

Traveling peddlers sold these drums, along with tops, kites, doll-like figures, and roly-poly tumblers. The roly-poly figures were made of wood, clay, and papier-mâché shaped like a person or animal. The bottom of the roly-poly was round and weighted, so it always bounced back to an upright position no matter how hard you pushed it over.

Traditionally, village craftsmen made toys by hand from natural materials such as bamboo, paper, cloth, silk, straw, and clay. At festival times, toy peddlers carrying their colorful wares would be surrounded by children. The peddler was laden with beautifully made pinwheels of paper and bamboo, Chinese "finger handcuffs" woven

The Chinese made toys, masks, and all kinds of other items out of papier-mâché. They also invented the first kites.

of reeds, toy swords with silk tassels, vividly colored clay men and animals, and carved whistles.

Some of these toys, enjoyed by children in China so long ago, were the forerunners of toys that children still play with today all over the world. Kites, puzzle rings, and yo-yos are all Chinese inventions.

Pets or Treats?

For a Chinese child with few toys, a hopping grasshopper, a lively cricket, or a buzzing dragonfly could make an exciting pet. The Chinese also liked to have cricket fights, a sport that exists to this day.

It wasn't easy to catch an insect like a cicada, high in a tree. To capture a cicada, children would put a sticky wad of homemade glue (made from rubber heated with cooking oil and mushed up) on the end of a long bamboo pole. Then they'd go "fishing" for cicadas.

After playing with these insect "airplanes," a child might roast it for a crunchy treat. Children also collected ants so that the family could enjoy ant soup!

After playing with a cicada, a child might roast and eat it!

Lotus Feet

In the 10th century, a dancer in the court of Emperor Li Yu danced on her toes like a ballerina. Other women wanted to look like her, which led to the custom of foot binding, a custom that lasted for a thousand years.

When girls were three to five years old, their mothers would wrap their feet tightly with a long white cloth. This bent their toes down, making their feet look like pointed lotus bulbs. People thought it was beautiful, but it was a cruel practice that kept the girls' feet from growing. As a result, women walked on painful doll-sized feet and suffered serious illnesses because of them.

Women always kept their bound feet covered. They were never allowed to be seen without shoes. Most women made their own tiny shoes, carefully embroidering them with Chinese good-luck symbols.

Some emperors made efforts to ban this cruel custom. But it wasn't until the Republic of China came into power in 1911 that it was stopped, ending more than 1,000 years of crippling pain.

Foot binding produced small but painfully deformed feet.

At School With Confucius

Confucius (Kong Fuzi or "Master Kong") was China's most famous philosopher. He was born in 551 B.C. At that time, most wealthy Chinese children, including daughters, learned how to read and write at home. Young men who had government positions received on-the-job training from their superior officers.

Confucius opened a school, but it was not like your school today. The students (young men, not boys or girls) had no classroom or textbooks. There was no homework or weekly tests. Confucius preferred to teach through conversations, either in a small group or with just one student. He asked questions and expected students to find their own answers. He insisted on honesty, alertness, and hard work.

Although he was a member of the upper class, Confucius admitted any young man who showed ability and a desire to learn. He conducted classes in his home, and some of his poorer students lived with him. According to legend, he taught a total of 3,000 pupils, but he rarely had more than 20 or 25 at any one time.

Besides learning to imitate Confucius' example, students also studied rituals, music, archery, calligraphy, arithmetic, and charioteering. A gentleman at that time was expected to be balanced.

Confucius wanted his students to develop compassion and respect for other people. He also wanted to prepare his students for government service. He thought that good officials would create good government and that good government would make for a peaceful society with happy people.

To achieve this, Confucius suggested a system of examinations. Whoever passed these tests would qualify for government service. China's leaders did not accept this idea immediately. Eventually they did, and Confucius is given credit as the inspiration behind China's examination system.

After his death, the sayings of Confucius were collected. These became the basis for moral and religious life in China. Although belief in Confucianism has declined, the teachings of Master Kong are still felt in China today.

Confucius taught small groups of students in his home. Today, his teachings are known around the world.

Bamboo Books & Word Pictures

Long before the invention of paper, the Chinese scratched characters onto bone, like this.

The books read by the students of Confucius looked very different from your schoolbooks today. The Chinese character for "book" looks like a bundle of long, narrow strips held together by a thin cord. That's what books were back then—bamboo strips with words carved on their surfaces. The strips were stacked up or joined like an accordion and then tied together with a cord of silk, hemp, or leather.

Scholars wrote their books with brushes made of bamboo or wood, and tips made of rabbit, goat, or deer hair. Ink was made by mixing water with soot from a fire.

To correct a mistake on bamboo, a writer would scrape the error off with a special knife called a *xue*. Whole layers could be shaved off and the strip used again.

Around A.D. 105, a court official named Cai Lun invented paper. Paper was made from a mushy pulp of wood, silk rags, bamboo, hemp, tree bark, or other fibers. The pulp was spread on a screen, then pressed flat and dried to make the paper. The use of paper quickly spread across China and helped advance Chinese culture.

What about the actual writing? Chinese handwriting dates back more than 3,000 years. The earliest surviving Chinese characters were scratched onto bones around

1200 B.C. Characters began as pictographs, or word pictures. For example, the ancient character for "water" resembled ripples of water. "Bird" was a stick-figure bird. These characters were used continuously until 221 B.C., when China was united for the first time. The first emperor, Shi-Huangdi, issued a standard set of characters to be used throughout the empire.

In ancient China, only rich boys learned to write. Students memorized dozens of characters each week. They painted word pictures with brushes and ink.

Chinese writing is done in columns of characters. The columns start in the upper right-hand corner, run down the page, and then across from right to left.

Modern Chinese writing has been simplified in the hope that the characters would be easier to learn. Although many characters have changed from their ancient forms, the traditional characters are still

Confucius read to his students from "books" made of strips of bamboo stacked and tied together.

19

Li

Ren

Xin

Yi

Zhi

in use in Taiwan, Hong Kong, and in China on occasion.

Although China's 1.2 billion people speak about 3,000 dialects, they use one written language. People in different parts of China, Japan, Korea, and Vietnam read the same characters and know what they mean, even though they pronounce the characters differently. Even though they don't speak the same language, people in China can always write something down if they are speaking to someone from a different part of the country or to someone from Japan or Korea or Vietnam, and they will be understood.

The Five Virtues of Confucius

Confucius believed that a man needed to practice five virtues to become a true "gentleman" and a good public official:

Li
Li, or "ritual etiquette" (manners), is the most important virtue.

Ren
Ren stands for "benevolence" or kindness toward others.

Xin
Xin stands for "faithfulness."

Yi
Yi stands for "righteousness" or honesty.

Zhi
Zhi stands for "knowledge" about right and wrong.

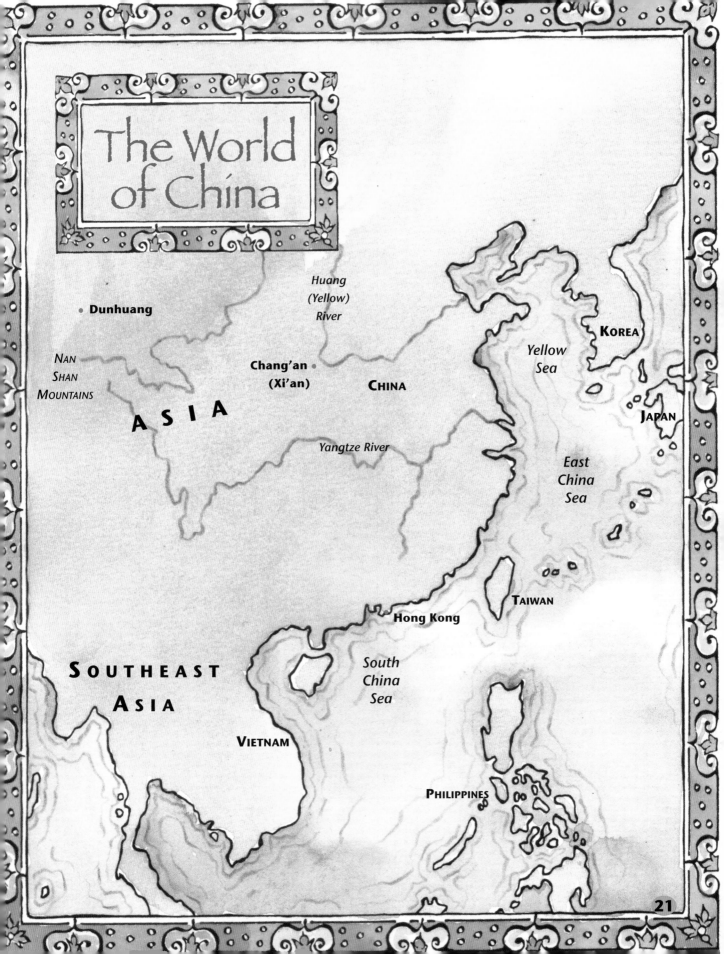

The World of China

Dunhuang

Huang (Yellow) River

Nan Shan Mountains

Chang'an (Xi'an)

CHINA

A S I A

Yangtze River

KOREA

Yellow Sea

JAPAN

East China Sea

S O U T H E A S T

A S I A

Hong Kong

TAIWAN

South China Sea

VIETNAM

PHILIPPINES

A Visit to Chang'an

Imagine living in the capital of China—not Beijing, the capital today, but Chang'an, which means "Perpetual Peace." At one time, it was the center of Chinese politics, culture, and trade.

Chang'an became China's first real capital city in 221 B.C., at the beginning of the Qin dynasty. It was one of the greatest and largest of the world's ancient cities. It was also the starting point for the Silk Road, the famous trade route between China and the markets of Central Asia and Europe.

You would probably feel safe living in Chang'an, since it was protected by walls that were 48 feet wide at the base! About 80,000 families lived within the city's walls. A Chinese poet once wrote that the houses in Chang'an were packed together "as closely as the teeth of a comb."

If you wanted to go shopping, you might go to one of the marketplaces located around the city. Here you would see travelers from all parts of Asia making deals or having their fortunes told.

Shops or stalls were laid out in rows, and vendors who sold the same types of goods competed with each other for customers. There were butcher shops, cooked-meat stalls, and sellers of syrup, pickled goods, dried fish, relishes, grains, and fruit. Hardware stores sold utensils and equipment made of brass, iron, and wood. Carriage makers proudly displayed their light two-wheeled vehicles and their heavier ox carts. Drapers sold rolls of fine silk and coarser fabrics of hemp, as well as furs.

Raw materials were also sold at the marketplaces, along with horses, cattle, sheep, and swine. Tax officials

Hist-O-Bit

Chang'an was built to face south, the direction that marked the sun's uppermost position in the heavens.

collected taxes on each day's transactions from their offices at the entrances to the marketplaces. The market was also the place where traitors and fallen statesmen were executed. At nightfall, the markets were closed to the public.

The streets of Chang'an were laid out in a grid, which divided the city into separate districts. Some of these housed palaces, others quarters for visitors, Buddhist monasteries, or residential areas for the general population. The design of the city symbolized the people's view of society as a series of interrelated groups, each placed in its own rightful position.

The city of Chang'an went through periods of growth and decline throughout China's history. Today, Chang'an is known as Xi'an, and travelers still come from all over the world to see sites such as the enormous tomb of Shi-Huangdi, the first emperor of China.

More than 8,000 life-size terra-cotta soldiers guard the tomb of Shi-Huangdi, first emperor of China.

Dynasties

China's long history can be broken down into dynasties, periods during which the country was ruled by one clan, or family. Here are the 11 major dynasties of China and what they are known for.

Xia (or Hsia)—2200–1766 B.C. The first dynasty, about which little is known.

Shang—1755–1040 B.C. Invention of bronze.

Zhou (or Chou)—1100–221 B.C.

Taoism and Confucianism begin.

Qin (or Ch'in)— 221–206 B.C. Great Wall of China begun.

Han—206 B.C.–A.D. 220 Many inventions; Buddhism begins.

Sui—A.D. 589–618 A short reign, with costly wars and huge public works projects such as canals.

Tang—A.D. 618–907 Includes the only female ruler in Chinese history, Wu Zhao.

Song (or Sung)— A.D. 960–1279 Poetry, painting, and education for nobles flourish.

Yuan—A.D. 1279–1368 Marco Polo visits China.

Ming—A.D. 1368–1644 Known for beautiful china pottery.

Qing (or Manchu)— A.D. 1644–1911 Last of the Chinese dynasties.

Along the Silk Road

My name is Fa Zang. I am 12 years old, and the year is A.D. 742. I am excited because I'm joining my father on my first caravan to a far-off city called Dunhuang. For trading, my father has porcelain, rhubarb, herbal medicine, and silk cloth, our most-prized item.

Our journey begins in Chang'an, where we live. Our caravan includes merchants such as my father, Chinese government officials, and, of course, camels. Camels may be slow, but they are sturdy animals that can carry our heavy loads.

We leave Chang'an and travel through the Wei River valley along the Imperial Highway. The landscape is bright green fields and mulberry trees. The ground is yellow with a fine dust that blows in the wind. If the wind is harsh, I will put a mask over my face, so the dust doesn't get inside my mouth or eyes.

At night, my feet are sore from walking. Our caravan stops at a shelter, so we don't have to sleep out in the open. Other traders are at the shelter, too. They have dates, pistachio nuts, peaches, and pears. Someone tosses me a pear. Its sweet, slippery juice drips down my chin while I eat it.

We continue on, stopping at farms for food along the way and meeting caravans coming and going. We travel through forests and hills, cross the Huang River, and trek the foothills of the Nan Shan Mountains. Finally, we reach Dunhuang, tired and sore from our long journey.

My father starts exchanging goods with caravans that have come from the West. He trades his silk for white jade and Persian metalwork. He trades the rhubarb for pistachio nuts and walnuts. He exchanges the herbal medicine for musical instruments. The government officials trade silk for horses for the emperor's army.

The men from the West describe unusual, foreign places on their journeys, such as Tyre and Byzantium. That night, I can barely sleep as thoughts of these exotic places fill my brain. But tomorrow, my father and I will travel back to Chang'an, so I must get my rest.

I dream of the travels yet to come.

Hist-O-Bit

Silk cloth, made from the cocoons of silkworms, was originally reserved for the emperors of China alone.

Religion on the Road

Silk, porcelain, spices, gold, and silver were not the only things transported along the Silk Road. Religious values and practices also spread along these routes.

In India, millions of people were Buddhists. The Buddha taught that life is suffering and that people should feel compassion for others and do as little harm as possible. Buddhist missionaries began to travel with merchants and adventurers along the Silk Road. Many merchants embraced the faith and gave money to support Buddhist monasteries, schools, and rest houses.

The main form of Christianity that moved eastward was Nestorianism. Many Nestorians had fled Constantinople because they disagreed with leaders of the Christian church there about the nature of Jesus, on whom Christianity is based. They built many churches in China during the era of the Silk Road.

Another important religion along the Silk Road was Zoroastrianism. Zoroaster, a Persian prophet, saw life as an eternal struggle between good (light) and evil (darkness). Those who sided with the good would be rewarded with eternal heaven; others would go to hell. Believers in Zoroastrianism frequently traveled along the trade routes, and a large group settled in India where their descendants continue to practice Zoroastrianism today.

A new faith that spread along the Silk Road was Manichaeism, which brought together Zoroastrianism and Christianity. It also absorbed aspects of Buddhism and took the idea of religious images from Hinduism.

Islam also played a significant role along the Silk Road. The faith had originated with nomadic groups in Arabia, and Arab Muslims quickly conquered many areas. Muhammad, Islam's prophet, had been a merchant, and Muslims were advised to "seek learning, even to China." As a result, traders and travelers played an important role in spreading the faith.

People who practiced different faiths interacted and influenced one another along the Silk Road. As they adopted new ideas and new religious beliefs, not only did they change, but the faiths changed as well. Many things were traded along the Silk Road, even religious ideas.

Glossary

Arabia Area of southwest Asia, location of Saudi Arabia today.

Archaeologist A person who studies ancient times by exploring fossils, relics, and ruins.

Buddhism Religion founded in India in the 6th century B.C. by Siddhartha Gautama, known as the Buddha.

Byzantium Capital of the Byzantine Empire, the successor to the Roman Empire, in present-day Istanbul, Turkey.

Calligraphy The art of fine lettering or handwriting.

Chinese characters The symbols used in Chinese writing.

Christianity Religion based on the life and teachings of Jesus and that believes he is the son of God.

Clan A group of people all descended from one individual.

Draper A person who sells cloth or clothing.

Dynasty A period of rule by a single family or clan.

Emperor Ruler of an empire.

Islam Religion that believes that Muhammad is the last and greatest prophet of God.

Manichaeism Religion that combines elements of Christianity, Zoroastrianism, and other religions.

Nestorianism Religion based on Christianity and that believes that Jesus had two distinct personalities, divine and human, rather than one.

Ocarina A small, egg-shaped musical instrument like a recorder, with a mouthpiece and finger holes.

Papier-mâché A pulp made of paper and glue, which can be molded into shapes.

Parchment Writing material made from the skins of sheep or goats.

Persia Ancient empire located in present-day Iran.

Pictograph A picture that represents a word or idea.

Porcelain White, hard ceramic material made of clay baked at high heat. Also called "china."

Republic of China The government formed in 1911, ending the rule of Chinese emperors.

Seismograph A device that detects movements in the ground, such as earthquakes.

Silk Road Ancient trading route that linked China to Europe.

Terra-cotta Rough ceramics, from the Latin words for "baked earth."

Tyre Capital and commercial center of ancient Phoenicia, an empire located in present-day Lebanon.

Zoroastrianism Religion that views life as an eternal struggle between light and darkness.

Index

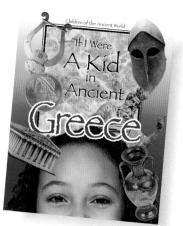
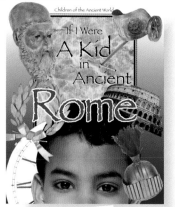
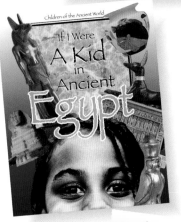

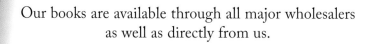